'One modern scholar on Galatians said that "Luther speaks as Paul would have spoken had he lived at the time Luther gave his lectures" (Hans Dieter Betz). Luther's great commentary speaks to us today and feeds our soul as well as teaching us Paul's theology in Galatians. I warmly recommend Lee Gatiss's work in making Luther's work available for us in the twenty-first century in such a winsome format.'

Rev. Dr. Rohintan Mody,
Director, North West Gospel Partnership

REFLECTING ON…

Galatians

with *Martin Luther*

Lee Gatiss

Scripture with the Saints
Reading the Bible with faithful believers across the ages

Reflecting on Galatians with Martin Luther
Scripture with the Saints

© Church Society 2025
Church Society
Ground Floor, Centre Block
Hille Business Estate,
132 St Albans Road
Watford WD24 4AE, UK

Tel +44 (0)1923 255410
www.churchsociety.org
admin@churchsociety.org

Unless otherwise stated, all Scripture quotations are taken from The Holy Bible, New International Version. Copyright © 1973, 1978, 1984, 2011 by Biblica, Inc. Used by permission. All rights reserved.

All rights reserved. Except as may be permitted by the Copyright Act, no part of this publication may be reproduced in any form or by any means without prior permission from the publisher.

Readers are reminded that the views expressed in this book do not necessarily represent those of Church Society.

Some of the studies in this book first appeared in *90 Days in Genesis, Exodus, Psalms, and Galatians with Calvin, Luther, Bullinger and Cranmer* by Lee Gatiss (Good Book Company, 2017).

Printed in the UK
ISBN: 978-1-0685705-2-0

Series Preface

Remember your leaders, who spoke the word of God to you. Consider the outcome of their way of life and imitate their faith. Jesus Christ is the same yesterday and today and forever. Do not be carried away by all kinds of strange teachings.

– Hebrews 13:7–9

The writer to the Hebrews encourages his listeners to remember their former Christian leaders who taught them the gospel and lived it out. We are urged elsewhere to honour our current spiritual guides (e.g. 1 Thessalonians 5:12–13), but here it seems to be former pastors that are in mind. As John Calvin (1509–1564) said, 'they who have begotten us in Christ ought to be to us in the place as it were of fathers', especially if they persevered to the end. So we are to imitate the way of life of these fathers in the faith and consider the outcome of their lives.

One good thing about learning from those who spoke the word of God and guided the church in the past is that we need have no fear that they will suddenly turn out to be rogues. Every generation has those who at a certain point swerve from the truth and upset the faith of some (see 2 Timothy 2:16–18). But we can see what the outcome of our fathers' way of life and teaching was, and how they served the same Saviour and Lord as we do today.

In an age which loves novelty, it is stabilising to consider the teaching and example of the saints who came before us. It can inoculate us against the strange teachings which vie for our attention in our own time, and help us to feed on more wholesome food. It can stir us up, correct us, rebuke us, and help us live out the unchanging gospel. This is not to commend superstitious devotion to the saints or romantic antiquarianism. Rather, it is to take seriously the charge to 'remember your leaders, who spoke the word of God to you.'

That's why in this series of short books we will be reflecting on the Bible together with trustworthy guides from church history who spoke the word of God. They will teach us, build us up in our ancient common faith, and bring the wisdom of the past into our daily lives. The word of God did not originate with us, and we are not the only ones it has reached! (1 Corinthians 14:36).

So I pray you will feel connected to your own spiritual family history as you sit down to study the Scriptures with some of the best guides from our past. They may see things in God's word which you had never noticed before. They may challenge you in ways you don't expect. And all they want in return is for you to follow Jesus Christ, who is the same yesterday, today, and forever – as they did.

How to use this book

Each day, this book gives you a passage of Scripture itself to read, and some questions to think about after you have done so. You will need your Bible open! It is good to reflect on what you have read in the word first, before moving on to see what others have said about it. Only after that will we have some guidance to ponder from our historical teacher. Their words are valuable only as they illuminate the unerring word of God itself and help us apply it to ourselves.

Following this, there will be some questions of application to think about. Spend some time meditating on how you can apply the word of God to your own life, in the light of what you have learned.

Finally, it is good to turn all this into prayer back to God. Spend some time talking to him about the lessons you learn in each day's reading. This will help you digest what you read and make it a part of your own walk with God.

There is a blank page after each day's feast, for you to record any reflections of your own, either in words or diagrams or drawings, as you feel led – whatever helps you remember and respond to the living word. What struck you most forcefully? What are you not sure about? What changes might this demand of you? How would you sum it all up? What should you pray for? In this way, this little book will also become a journal of your own daily dealings with God.

I hope you will feel invigorated, challenged, comforted, and urged on in your Christian life by reading Scripture with the saints. And most of all, that you will enjoy getting to know Christ better and growing in your love and appreciation for him.

LEE GATISS
Series Editor

Martin Luther

Martin Luther (1483–1546) kickstarted the Protestant Reformation by posting his Ninety-five Theses against the Roman Catholic practice of indulgences on the door of the Castle Church in Wittenberg on 31st October, 1517. Or so the story goes. A German monk turned university lecturer, Luther had a fiery personality and a penetrating intellect, and his refusal to retract his early writings led to his excommunication by the Pope in 1521. He translated the Bible into vernacular German, and continued to teach theology at Wittenberg until he died in his hometown of Eisleben in 1546. His complete works run to 121 volumes, spanning about eighty thousand pages.

This book features extracts from Luther's commentary on Galatians, transcribed from his lectures given in 1531 and first published in Latin in 1535. I have freely modernised and updated the 1575 English translation. 'The Epistle to the Galatians is my epistle,' Luther once said. 'I am betrothed to it. It is my Katie von Bora.' Since he compared it to his beloved wife, it is safe to say that he felt a special affinity for Galatians, and his comments on it contain many of his key Reformation insights.

�֎ Day 1 ֎

Sent by Jesus

GALATIANS 1:1–5

We begin by tucking into the work of Martin Luther on Galatians – 'my dear epistle' as he called it.

Read Galatians 1:1–5

Why do you think Paul insists so strongly that his ministry is 'not from men' (verse 1)?

Does Paul mention his status for his own glory or for some other reason, do you think?

Paul's calling

When Paul so highly commends his calling, he is not seeking his own praise. But with a necessary and a holy pride he magnifies his ministry. That is to say, *I want people to receive me, not as Paul of Tarsus, but as Paul the apostle and ambassador of Jesus Christ.* And he does this to maintain his authority, that the people, in hearing this, might be more attentive and willing to give ear to him.

This is the first assault that Paul makes against the false apostles, who ran when no one sent them. Calling, therefore, is not to be despised. For it is not enough for someone to have the word and pure doctrine, but they must also be assured of their calling. So our fantastical spirits at this day have the words of faith in their mouths, but yet they yield no fruit, for their chief end and purpose is to draw people to their false and perverse opinions.

The seriousness of word ministry

This then is our comfort, that we who are in the ministry of the word have an office which is heavenly and holy. Being lawfully called to this, we triumph against all the gates of hell. We see then how good and necessary Paul's boasting is.

In times past when I was a young theologian and teacher, I thought Paul was unwise to glory so often in his calling in all his epistles. But I did not understand his purpose. For I did not know that the ministry of God's word was so weighty a matter. I knew nothing of the doctrine of faith, because there was then no certainty taught either in the universities or churches, but all was full of the clever subtleties of academics. And therefore no-one was able to understand the dignity and power of this holy and spiritual boasting. True and lawful calling serves, first, to the glory of God and, secondly, to the advancing of our office. Moreover, it also serves to the salvation of ourselves and of the people.

Apply

Would it be right to think of Paul's letters as 'just his opinion' or as simply a record of his experience of the grace of God? If not, why not?

Given that they are not apostles as Paul was, how should we think of those who teach and preach the Bible today? Do you think Luther is right to draw some comparisons between them?

Pray

Pray that you would listen attentively to Paul's teaching from Galatians, as a gift to us from God.

Pray too for those who preach and teach in your church, that they would know the weightiness of their calling, and do everything for God's glory.

NOTES AND PRAYERS

�֍ Day 2 ✶

Christ Gave Himself

GALATIANS 1:1–5

Today we look at a verse that Luther said was 'a singular comfort to those who are terrified by the greatness of their sins'.

Read Galatians 1:1–5 again

What is the link between verses 3 and 4?

Why do you think Paul includes verse 4 in his opening greeting?

Christ has given himself

Paul has nothing in his mouth but Christ, and therefore in every word there is a fervency of spirit and life. Mark how well and to the purpose he speaks. He does not say Christ, 'who has *received* our works at our hands', nor 'who has received the sacrifices of Moses' law, worshippings, religions, masses, vows, and pilgrimages'.

No. Christ has *given*. What has he given? Not gold nor silver, nor beasts, nor Passover lambs, nor an angel, but himself. For what? Not for a crown; not for a kingdom; not for our holiness or righteousness – but for our sins.

These words are very thunder claps from heaven against all kinds of righteousness. Therefore we must with diligent attention mark Paul's every word, and not slenderly consider them or lightly pass them over. For they are full of consolation, and confirm fearful consciences exceedingly.

Satisfaction for sin

How may we obtain forgiveness of our sins? Paul answers that the man called Jesus Christ, the Son of God, has given himself for them. These are excellent and most comfortable words – our sins are taken away by no other means than by the Son of God delivered unto death. With such guns and such artillery must the system of our opponents be destroyed, and all the religions of the heathen, all works, all merits and all superstitious ceremonies. For if our sins may be taken away by our own works, merits and satisfactions, why did the Son of God need to be given up for them?

But seeing that he was given for them, it follows that we cannot do away with them by our own works. Again, by this sentence it is declared that our sins are so great, so infinite and invincible, that it is impossible for the whole world to satisfy for one of them.

And surely the greatness of the ransom (namely Christ, the Son of God, who gave himself for our sins) declares sufficiently that we can neither satisfy for sin, nor have dominion over it.

Apply

Is it a comfort to you that, rather than demanding something for your sins, Christ gave himself for them? If not, why not?

How awful must our sins be that the only remedy for them was for Christ, the Son of God, to give himself up to death for them? Do you think of your sins in this way?

Pray

Praise God for his grace towards us in sending Jesus to die in our place on the cross.

Thank Jesus for rescuing us from the present evil age, which has been ruined by sin and is under God's curse.

NOTES AND PRAYERS

❊ Day 3 ❊

Falling Away is Easy

Galatians 1:6–10

Congregations which are won by great labour may easily and quickly be overthrown, so we ought carefully to watch out for the devil, lest he sneaks in while we sleep.

Read Galatians 1:6–10

How did Paul feel about the churches he had planted deserting the gospel?

How had this happened?

Overturning the gospel

See how Paul complains that to fall and to err in the faith is an easy matter. A minister may labour ten years to get some little church to be rightly and religiously ordered; and when it is so ordered, there creeps in some mad, unlearned idiot, who knows nothing but how to speak slanderously against the sincere preachers of the word, and they in one moment overthrow all.

We by the grace of God have gotten here at Wittenberg the form of a Christian church. The word is purely taught among us, the sacraments are rightly used, and all things go forward prosperously. This most happy course of the gospel some mad head would soon stop, and in one moment would overturn all that we in many years have built with great labour.

This happened even to Paul, the elect vessel of Christ. He had won the churches of Galatia with great care, but in a short time after his departure the false apostles overthrew them. We so walk in the midst of Satan's snares that one fantastical head may destroy in a short space all that which many true ministers, labouring night and day, have built up.

Caring for the church

Seeing then that the church is so soft and so tender a thing, and is so soon overthrown, we must watch carefully against these fantastical spirits, who, when they have heard a few sermons or have read a few pages in the holy Scriptures, make themselves masters and controllers of all learners and teachers, contrary to common authority.

At the first, when the light of the gospel began to appear, after such a great darkness of human traditions, many were zealously bent to godliness. They heard sermons greedily and had the ministers of God's word in reverence. But now, when the doctrine of piety and godliness is happily reformed, with so great an increase of God's word, many which before seemed earnest disciples become despisers and very enemies. They not only cast off the study of God's word, and despise its ministers, but also hate all good learning.

Apply

First, we must watch ourselves. Are you still zealous for the true gospel message and keen to pass it on faithfully?

Second, what can you do to help ensure that your church does not turn away to a different gospel?

Pray

Pray for your own heart to remain faithful to the true gospel.

Pray that false teaching does not enter your church; and that if it does, it is driven away by faithful ministers.

Notes and prayers

✷ Day 4 ✷

To the Glory of God Alone

Galatians 1:11–24

Don't believe Luther, or the church, or the fathers, or the apostles – not even an angel from heaven if they teach anything against the revealed word of God.

Read Galatians 1:11–24

Where did Paul's gospel come from (verses 11–12)?

Why do you think Paul talks about the journeys he made after his conversion?

The gospel came from God

Paul says he did not learn his gospel from any man, but received it by a revelation. But the matter of justification is fickle – not of itself (for of itself it is most sure and certain) – but in respect of us.

I myself have good experience of this. For I know in what hours of darkness I sometimes wrestle. I know how often suddenly I lose the beams of the gospel and grace, as being shadowed from me with thick and dark clouds.

I know in what a slippery place others who seem to have sure footing in matters of faith also do stand. In respect of us, it is a very fickle matter, because we are fickle. Therefore we teach continually that the knowledge of Christ and of faith is no work of man, but simply the gift of God. As he creates faith, so does he keep it in us.

Giving all glory to God

I attribute all things to God alone, and nothing to man. When I first took upon me the defence of the gospel, I remember that a worthy man said to me, 'I really like that this doctrine which you preach yields all glory to God alone, and nothing to man: for to God there cannot be attributed too much glory, goodness, and mercy'. This saying greatly comforted and confirmed me. And it is true that the doctrine of the gospel takes from men all glory, wisdom and righteousness, and gives them to the Creator alone.

It is much safer to attribute too much to God than to man. For in this case I may say boldly: Even if the church, Augustine and other doctors, Peter and Apollos – yes, even an angel from heaven – teach a contrary doctrine, yet my doctrine is such, that it sets forth and preaches the grace and glory of God alone. And in the matter of salvation, it condemns the righteousness and wisdom of all. In this case I cannot offend, because I give both to God and man that which properly and truly belongs to them both.

Apply

Does your confidence as a Christian come from the gospel revelation itself or from some other source (such as your church, your camp, your pastor, your knowledge, your credentials)?

When church people let you down, or you struggle to believe, do you turn back to the revelation of God in the Bible, or to something else?

Pray

Thank God that the good news of Jesus has been proclaimed to you, and that he gave you faith to believe it.

Ask God to help you continue trusting in his gospel rather than in any merely human authority.

Notes and prayers

�֎ Day 5 �֎

By Faith Alone

Galatians 2:1–10

We should not allow our consciences to be bound to any 'work', so that by doing this thing or that we consider ourselves righteous, or by leaving it undone we think we are damned.

Read Galatians 2:1–10

Why was it so important to Paul that Titus was not forced to be circumcised (verses 3–5)?

What liberating truth of the gospel was Paul trying to defend against the 'you must be circumcised' group (verse 5)?

The place of circumcision

Paul did not reject circumcision as a damnable thing. Neither did he, by word or deed, force the Jews to forsake it. But he rejected circumcision as a thing not necessary to righteousness. The Old Testament patriarchs themselves were not justified by circumcision, but for them it was only a sign or a seal of righteousness by which they showed and exercised their faith.

Hearing that circumcision was not necessary for righteousness, the believing Jews who were still weak and had a zeal for the Old Testament law thought this meant that it was altogether unprofitable and damnable. And the false apostles only encouraged this fond opinion, so that the hearts of the people would be stirred up by this against Paul, and so they might thoroughly discredit his doctrine.

Similarly, we today do not reject fasting and other good exercises as damnable things. But we do teach that by these exercises we do not obtain forgiveness of sins. When the people hear this, they judge us to speak against good works. But for many years past there has been none that has more truly and faithfully taught concerning good works than we do!

Faith alone

Now the *truth* of the gospel is that our righteousness comes by faith *only* – without the works of the law. The *corruption* of the gospel is that we are justified by faith, but not without also doing the works of the law. With conditions like these, the false apostles also preached their gospel.

Others preach in the same way today. For they say that we must believe in Christ, and that faith is the foundation of our salvation – but it does not justify someone, unless it is also furnished with love. This is not the truth of the gospel, but falsehood and misrepresentation. The true gospel is that works or love are not the ornament or perfection of faith, but that faith itself is God's gift and God's work in our hearts, which therefore justifies us because it takes hold of Christ our redeemer.

Apply

Is there any good work or good cause that people say (or imply) you have to embrace to be a 'proper Christian'? Is it right to add that as a requirement to 'faith alone'?

Is it just 'being picky' to insist that justification is by faith alone?

Pray

Praise God that through the gospel we are justified by faith alone, which is his gift.

Ask God to help you speak about this issue clearly and defend it.

Notes and prayers

✻ Day 5 ✻

Not by Works

Galatians 2:11–21

It is a horrible blasphemy to imagine that there is any work by which you could presume to pacify God.

Read Galatians 2:11–21

Note: Cephas is another name for Peter.

Why was Peter's behaviour not in line with the gospel (verse 14)?

How does Paul describe the true Christian life in these verses?

True religion

Paul briefly summarised the principal article of all Christian doctrine, which makes true Christians indeed, when he said, 'We [are] justified by faith and not by the works of the law'. This our opponents do not believe, but continue to say, 'Whoever does this good work or that deserves forgiveness of sins', or 'Whoever enters into this or that holy order, and keeps this rule, to him we assuredly promise everlasting life'.

But if no flesh is justified by the works of the law, much less shall it be justified by the Rule of Benedict, Francis, or Augustine, in which there is not one jot of true faith in Christ; but this only they urge, that whoever keeps these things has life everlasting.

I have often marvelled how the true church could endure and continue as it has done, since these destructive heresies have reigned for so many years in such great darkness and errors. But there were some whom God called by the letter of the gospel and by baptism. These walked in simplicity and humbleness of heart, thinking that the monks and friars, and such only as were anointed by the bishops, were religious and holy, and they themselves were profane and secular, and not worthy to be compared to them. Therefore, finding in themselves no good works to set against the wrath and judgment of God, they did fly to the death and passion of Christ, and were saved in this simplicity.

Christian righteousness

But this we may plainly see, that there is nothing here for us *to do*. It belongs to us, rather, only to hear that these things have been *done* for us, and by faith to grasp hold of them.

In verse 20, Paul says, 'I no longer live, but Christ lives in me'. Here he plainly shows by what means he lives. He teaches what true Christian righteousness is, namely the righteousness by which Christ lives in us, and not that which is in our own person. Christ is my righteousness and life.

Apply

What do you think a really good Christian life looks like? Would Luther or Paul agree?

What barriers do we put in the way of other Christians, or what hoops do we make them jump through to be truly accepted?

Pray

Praise 'the Son of God, who loved me and gave himself for me' (verse 20).

Ask the Lord to show you how to live for God by faith in Jesus, without trusting in your own works or insisting that others do them too.

Notes and prayers

❊ Day 7 ❊

He Loved Me

Galatians 2:20

Just as Christ was crucified to the law, sin, death, and the devil, so that they have no more power over him, so also I – through faith – am crucified with him, and they have no power over me either.

Read Galatians 2:20

If you knew you were going to die today, what would your first thoughts be about?

How close are you to Jesus?

Turn your eyes to him, not yourself

Such is our misery, that when temptation or death come, we set Christ aside and start considering our own past and the things we have done. Unless we are raised up again by faith, we will certainly perish. So we must learn in such conflicts and terrors of conscience to forget ourselves, and set aside the law, our past life, and all our works which drive us only to consider ourselves. We must turn our eyes wholly to Jesus Christ crucified, and assuredly believe that he is our righteousness and life, not fearing the threatenings and terrors of law, sin, death, and the judgment of God. For Christ, on whom our eyes are fixed, in whom we live, who also lives in us, is lord and conqueror of the law, sin, death, and all evils. So, Christ living and abiding in me, takes away and swallows up all evils which vex and afflict me.

You are joined to Christ

You are so entirely and closely joined to Christ that he and you are, as it were, made one person. You may boldly say, 'I am now one with Christ.' That is to say, Christ's righteousness, victory, and life are mine. And again, Christ may say, 'I am that sinner, that is, his sins and his death are mine, because he is united and joined to me, and I to him.' This faith couples Christ and me more closely together than a husband is coupled to his wife.

These words, 'the Son of God loved me, and gave himself for me' are mighty thunderings and lightnings from heaven against the righteousness of the law and all its works. Such great and such horrible wickedness, error, darkness, and ignorance were in my will and understanding, that it was impossible for me to be ransomed by any other means than by such an inestimable price. There is nothing which is able to pacify God but this – one drop of his blood is more precious than the whole world.

Apply

Think of all the ways in which Christ is perfect and sufficient. How amazing is it that he loved you, even to death?

How would it change the way you think about sin and temptation, if you thought more often in the moment about your union with Christ?

Pray

Praise God that he took the initiative to save us through the cross, rather than waiting for us to make the first move.

Ask God to help you consider yourself united to Christ more closely than a husband and wife.

Notes and prayers

✣ Day 8 ✣

Righteous Sinners

Galatians 3:1–9

It is an unspeakable gift that God accepts us as righteous without works, when we embrace his Son by faith alone – even our imperfect faith.

Read Galatians 3:1–9

How is the way we begin the Christian life related to the way we continue (verses 2–5)?

What do Christian believers have in common with Abraham (verses 6–9)?

God accepts my imperfect faith

Let those who study the word of God learn from this saying: 'Abraham believed God, and it was credited (counted) to him as righteousness'. This sets forth rightly what true Christian righteousness is – a faith and confidence in the Son of God, or rather a confidence of the heart in God through Jesus Christ.

This faith and confidence is accounted righteousness for Christ's sake. For these two things work Christian righteousness: namely, faith in the heart, which is a gift of God and rightly believes in Christ; and also, that God accepts this imperfect faith for perfect righteousness, for the sake of Christ, in whom I have come to believe.

Because of this faith in Christ, God does not see my doubting of his good will towards me, my distrust, my heaviness of spirit, and other sins which are yet in me. For as long as I live in the flesh, sin is truly in me. But because I am covered under the shadow of Christ's wings, as is the chicken under the wing of the hen, God covers and pardons the remnant of sin in me. That is to say, because of that faith by which I began to lay hold on Christ, he accepts my imperfect righteousness even for perfect righteousness, and counts my sin for no sin, even though it is sin indeed.

Righteous and sinful simultaneously

Thus a Christian is both righteous and a sinner, holy and profane, an enemy of God and yet a child of God. Our opponents cannot accept these paradoxes, for they do not know the true manner of justification. And this is why they make people work hard until they should feel no sin at all in them – and thereby they give occasion to many to become stark mad. Many of them, striving (unsuccessfully) with all their endeavour to be perfectly righteous, at the point of death were driven into desperation. Which would have happened to me also, if Christ had not mercifully looked on me and helped me out of this error.

Apply

Be comforted by the fact that, when you are a Christian, God accepts even your imperfect and wavering faith and counts it as righteousness.

Rejoice that you can be counted as completely right with God even though you are still a sinner.

Pray

Pray for any you know who are stuck in the error of thinking they have to be perfectly righteous in themselves in order to be acceptable to God.

Praise and thank God that he covers and forgives your sin, even your distrust, and accepts your imperfect faith.

Notes and prayers

�֎ Day 9 ✼

The Happy Exchange

GALATIANS 3:10–14

Making a happy exchange with us, Christ took upon himself our sinful person, and gave to us his innocent and victorious person.

Read Galatians 3:10–14

Why is there a curse on people who rely on the law to save them (verses 10–11)?

How did Christ become a curse for us (verse 13)?

Punished in my place

Christ is innocent as concerning his own person, and therefore he ought not to have been hanged upon a cross. But because, according to the law of Moses, every thief ought to be hanged, therefore

Christ also according to the law ought to be hanged, for he took the person of a sinner and of a thief – not of one, but of all sinners and thieves. For we are sinners and thieves, and therefore guilty of death and everlasting damnation. But Christ took all our sins upon him, and for them died upon the cross.

Christ was not only crucified and died, but sin also (through the divine love) was laid upon him. When sin was laid upon him, then along comes the law and says, 'Every sinner must die. Therefore, O Christ, if you become guilty and suffer punishment for sinners, you must also bear sin and curse.'

Because he had taken upon himself our sins, not by constraint, but of his own good will, it was fitting for him to bear the punishment and wrath of God – not for his own person (which was just and invincible, and therefore could in no way be found guilty) but for us.

Not merely an example

Some try to rob us of this knowledge of Christ and this most heavenly comfort when they separate him from sins and sinners, and only set him forth to us as an example to be followed. But we must know him to be wrapped in our sins, in our curse, in our death, and in all our evils, just as he is wrapped in our flesh and in our blood.

Let us therefore receive this doctrine, which is most sweet and full of comfort with thanksgiving, and with an assured faith – a faith which teaches that Christ being made a curse for us (that is, a sinner subject to the wrath of God) did put upon him our person, and laid our sins upon his own shoulders, saying, 'I have committed the sins which all men have committed'.

Apply

Meditate on the humility and grace of Christ that he stooped so very low, wrapping himself in our flesh and blood so he could wrap himself in our sin and curse.

Ponder how we would have to bear the wrath and curse of God if Jesus had not done it for us.

Pray

Praise God that Jesus took the punishment for your sins and bore God's wrath in your place.

Thank God for the comfort of having Jesus not just as an example to follow but as a Saviour who put himself in harm's way for us.

Notes and prayers

�֎ Day 10 �֎

A Sure Inheritance

Galatians 3:15–20

If a person's 'last will and testament' is faithfully executed and not added to after they die, how much more should the last will of God, be faithfully kept, which he promised to Abraham and his Seed and was confirmed in Christ's death.

Read Galatians 3:15–20

How would you feel if you inherited £1 million, but a lawyer then added an impossible legal requirement to the will, after your generous benefactor's will had been read?

Why do you think Paul adds a worldly illustration at this point in his teaching, designed to outrage us by its obvious unfairness?

God's will

The last will and testament (or covenant) of God was confirmed by the death of Christ. Therefore, no-one ought to change it or add anything to it, which those who teach the law and human traditions do. For they say that unless you are circumcised, keep the law, do many works, and suffer many things, you cannot be saved. This is not the last will and testament of God. For he did not say to Abraham, 'If you do this or that you will obtain the blessing.' But he said, 'In your Seed shall all the nations of the earth be blessed.' As if he should say, 'I, of mere mercy, do promise to you that Christ shall come from your seed, and bring blessing to all the nations oppressed with sin and death. He shall deliver the nations from the everlasting curse, from sin and death, when they receive this promise by faith.'

God's promise

Here, he calls the promises of God, that Christ would bring blessing to all nations, a testament. Now, a testament is not a law, but a donation or free gift. For heirs look not for laws, exactions, or any burdens to be laid upon them by a testament, but they look for the inheritance confirmed by it. The law, says Paul, was given four hundred and thirty years after this promise was made, and it could not make the promise void and unprofitable. God promised and confirmed it, and it remains ratified and sure for ever.

The law was not added so that the posterity of Abraham could obtain the blessing through it. It was added so that there might be in the world a certain people, with the word and testimony of Christ, out of which Christ might be born according to the flesh. And that people, bring kept and shut up under the law, might sigh and groan for their deliverance through the Seed of Abraham, which is Christ. The ceremonies commanded in the law foreshadowed

Christ. So the promise is not abolished by the law. Abraham didn't obtain righteousness through the law, but through mere promise.

Apply

What would you say to people who want to add various requirements and laws for you to keep in order to be saved? How does Paul's analogy in this passage help to answer them?

How incredible is it to think that God promised you an inheritance by grace even 2000 years before Jesus came? What should your response be to this?

Pray

Praise God for an inheritance that you could never earn and did not deserve, which is safe and secure.

Ask God to help you enjoy that promised blessing without the burden of man-made rules and regulations to keep.

Notes and prayers

�֍ Day 11 ✶

Children of God

Galatians 3:21–29

The true use of the Old Testament law is to teach us, so that we are brought to the knowledge of our sin and humbled, that we may come to Christ and be children of God.

Read Galatians 3:21–29

What does it mean for the law to be a guardian or schoolmaster (verses 24–25)?

Why is being a child of God such an amazing blessing (verses 26–29)?

The law as our schoolmaster

A schoolmaster is appointed to teach children, to bring them up, and to keep them, as it were, in prison. But to what end, or how long? Is it to the end that this sharp dealing of the schoolmaster should always continue? Or that the child should remain in continual bondage? Not so, but only for a time, that this obedience, this prison and correction might turn to the profit of the child, that in time they might be heir and prince.

For it is not a father's will that his child should be always subject to the schoolmaster, and always beaten with rods – but that by this instruction and discipline they may be made fit and able to be the father's successor. Even so the law (says Paul) is nothing else but a schoolmaster – not for ever, but until it has brought us to Christ.

By this, Paul shows us what the true use of the law is – namely, that it does not justify hypocrites, for they remain without Christ in their presumption and security; but rather, that it does not leave those who are of a contrite heart in death and damnation, but drives them to Christ.

The blessing of adoption

Paul does not say, 'You are the children of God because you are circumcised, because you have heard the law and have done its works' (as the Jews do imagine, and the false apostles teach) – but 'by faith in Jesus Christ'. The law then does not make us the children of God, and much less do human traditions.

Faith in Christ makes us the children of God, and not the law. What tongue either of men or angels can sufficiently extol and magnify the great mercy of God towards us, that we who are miserable sinners and by nature the children of wrath, should be called to this grace and glory? We are made the children and heirs of God, fellow heirs with the Son of God, and lords over heaven and earth, and that only by means of our faith which is in Christ Jesus.

Apply

Do you appreciate how great a blessing it is to be considered a child of God, by faith alone? How do you show your appreciation?

Does the law, when it reveals your sin and humbles you, make you turn to Christ for forgiveness, or drive you into despair?

Pray

Praise God for turning us from children of wrath into children of God, not by imposing on us the weighty law, but simply by faith in Jesus.

Ask God to give you a contrite heart which humbly rejoices in the blessing of being his child.

Notes and Prayers

�֍ Day 12 �֍

The Spirit and the Word

Galatians 4:1–11

When we willingly and gladly hear the word about Christ preached, be assured that God, by and with this preaching, sends the Holy Spirit into our hearts.

Read Galatians 4:1–11

What are the benefits of being a child of God?

How does being a child of God affect our relationship to the law?

Signs of the Spirit

The Holy Spirit is sent by the word into the hearts of believers. This sending is without any visible appearance; rather, by the hearing of the external word, we receive an inward fervency and light – by which we are changed and become new creatures, and receive a new mind, a new feeling, and a new moving. This change is the gift and operation of the Holy Spirit, which comes with the word preached, which purifies our hearts by faith, and brings forth in us spiritual motions.

And although it may not appear to the world that we are renewed in spirit and have the Holy Spirit, yet our speech and our confession do declare sufficiently that the Holy Spirit with his gifts is in us.

We ought not therefore to doubt whether the Holy Spirit dwells in us or not, but to be assuredly persuaded that we are the temple of the Holy Spirit, as Paul says (1 Corinthians 3:16; 6:19). For if anyone feels in themselves a love towards the word of God, and willingly hears, talks, writes and thinks of Christ, let that person know that this is not the work of human will or reason, but the gift of the Holy Spirit. For it is impossible that these things should be done without the Holy Spirit.

Contempt for the word

On the other hand, where there is hatred and contempt for the word, there the devil (the god of this world) reigns, blinding people's hearts and holding them captive, that the gospel – the glory of Christ – should not shine on them (2 Corinthians 4:4). Which is what we see at this day in the majority of people, who have no love for the word but presumptuously treat it with contempt as though it had nothing at all to do with them.

But whoever feels any love or desire for the word, let them acknowledge with thankfulness that this affection is poured into them by the Holy Spirit. For we are not born with this affection and desire.

Apply

Does your speech 'sufficiently declare' that the Holy Spirit is in you? Why / why not?

Do you love the word of God and willingly hear, talk, and think of Christ?

Pray

Pray that the Holy Spirit would fan into flame your love for his word.

Pray for those who treat God's word with contempt, including any you know personally, that the Spirit would open the eyes of their hearts to it.

Notes and prayers

❋ Day 13 ❋

Patience and Perplexity

Galatians 4:12–20

Paul used sweet and gentle words so that if he had offended anyone he might win them back to the truth again by these loving words and fatherly affection.

Read Galatians 4:12–20

Why is Paul perplexed about the Galatians (verse 20)?

What had changed their attitude towards him (verse 17)?

Patient pastoring

By his own example, Paul admonishes all pastors and ministers, that they ought to have a fatherly and motherly affection – not towards ravening wolves, but towards the poor sheep who are miserably seduced and going astray, patiently bearing with their faults and infirmities, instructing and restoring them with the spirit of meekness. For they cannot be brought into the right way again by any other means. By overly sharp reproving and rebuking they are provoked to anger, or else to desperation, but not to repentance.

Error creates disunity

Such is the nature and fruit of true and sound doctrine that when it is well taught and well understood, it joins people's hearts together with a singular concord. But when people reject godly and sincere doctrine, and embrace errors, this unity and concord is soon broken. Therefore as soon as you see your brethren seduced (by vain and fantastical spirits) to fall from the doctrine of justification, you will perceive that by and by they will pursue the faithful with bitter hatred, whom before they most tenderly loved.

This we find to be true at this day in our false brethren and other breakaway groups, who at the beginning of the reformation of the gospel were glad to hear us and read our books with great zeal and affection. They acknowledged the grace of the Holy Spirit in us, and reverenced us for that as the ministers of God. Some of them also lodged with us for a time. But when they departed from us and were perverted by the wicked doctrine of the breakaway groups, they showed themselves more bitter enemies to our doctrine and our name than any other.

I do much and often marvel why they should conceive such a deadly hatred against us, whom they before so dearly and so tenderly loved. Even they are constrained to confess that we desire nothing more than that the glory of God may be advanced and the truth of the gospel purely taught – which God has now again in these latter days revealed by us to this ungrateful world.

Apply

Why do you think is it hard to be patient and meek with those who seem to be wandering away from the gospel?

How true is it that people who once embraced but then move away from the gospel message Luther is talking about often become bitter enemies of it?

Pray

Pray that God would give you patience and gentleness in your relationships with those who seem to be wandering from the truth.

Ask God to keep your church faithful to and united in the truth of the gospel.

Notes and prayers

❊ Day 14 ❊

Persecution

Galatians 4:21–31

There will always be persecution in the church, especially when the doctrine of the gospel flourishes. The 'children of the flesh' mock the 'children of the promise'.

Read Galatians 4:21–31

Why do you think Paul uses an example from Genesis to try and persuade his readers?

Why is it significant that Hagar's child (Ishmael, here in Galatians 4 representing those who seek salvation through works) persecuted Sarah's (Isaac, representing those who trust in God's salvation promises) (verse 29)?

Persecution is inevitable

This passage contains a singular consolation. Whoever is born and lives in Christ, and rejoices in this birth and inheritance of

God, has Ishmael for their enemy and their persecutor. This we learn today by experience: for we see that all the world is full of tumults, persecutions, and breakaway groups. If we did not arm ourselves with this consolation of Paul, and well understand this doctrine of justification, we should never be able to withstand the violence and subtle sleights of Satan.

Truly, it is no small grief to us when we are forced to hear that all things were in peace and tranquillity before the gospel came, and that since the preaching and publishing of it, all things are unquiet and the whole world is in an uproar. When someone who is not endued with the Spirit of God hears this, they are offended and judge that infinite evils do proceed directly from the doctrine of the gospel.

Against this great offence we must comfort and arm ourselves with this sweet consolation, that the faithful must bear this name and this title in the world – that they are troublemakers who promote division, and the authors of innumerable evils. This is why our adversaries think they have a just cause, and even that they do God high service, when they hate, persecute and kill us.

Enduring persecution

It is inevitable then, that Ishmael must persecute Isaac. But Isaac does not persecute Ishmael. Whoever will not suffer the persecution of Ishmael, let them not profess to be a Christian. Whoever wants to preach Christ truly, and confess him to be our righteousness, must be content to hear that they are a pernicious fellow.

Such tumults and hurly-burlies we hear and see at this day. The adversaries lay the fault in our doctrine. But the doctrine of grace and peace does not stir up these troubles. Moreover, the doctrine for which they raise up such tumults is not ours, but it is the doctrine of Christ. This doctrine we cannot deny, nor give up the defence of it (Luke 9:26).

Apply

What would you say to someone who claimed the Reformation was a huge tragedy because it divided the church?

What would you say to someone who asked, 'Why can't Christians all just get along?'

Pray

Pray for those who face serious and violent persecution for being Christians, that they would stand firm in their faith.

Pray for those who persecute Christians, especially those who are themselves within the church, that God would grant them repentance and a knowledge of the truth.

Notes and Prayers

✷ Day 15 ✷

Spiritual Liberty

Galatians 5:1–6

Instead of sin and death, Christ gives us righteousness and everlasting life, changing the bondage and terrors of the law into liberty of conscience and gospel consolation.

Read Galatians 5:1–6

What do you think it means in verse 1 that Christ has set us free?

What would the opposite of that freedom be?

Freedom from fear

This passage speaks of that liberty by which Christ has made us free – not from an earthly bondage, or from the Babylonian captivity, or from the tyranny of the Turkish Muslim empire, but from God's everlasting wrath. For Christ has made us free, not civilly nor bodily, but divinely. That is to say, we are made free in such a way that our conscience is now free and quiet, not fearing the wrath of God to come.

Who is able to express what a thing it is when a man is assured in his heart that God neither is nor will be angry with him, but will be for ever a merciful and a loving Father to him for Christ's sake? This is indeed a marvellous and an incomprehensible liberty, to have the most high and sovereign Majesty so favourable to us that he does not only defend, maintain and support us in this life, but also, as touching our bodies, will so deliver us that our bodies, which are sown in corruption, in dishonour and infirmity, shall rise again in incorruption, in glory and power. This is an inestimable liberty, that we are made free from the wrath of God for ever.

Liberty from the law

Let us learn therefore to magnify this our liberty purchased by Jesus Christ, the Son of God, by whom all things were created both in heaven and earth. This liberty he has purchased with no other price than with his own blood, to deliver us not from any bodily or earthly servitude, but from a spiritual and everlasting bondage under mighty and invincible tyrants – that is, the law, sin, death and the devil – and so to reconcile us to God his Father.

Now, since these enemies are overcome, and we are reconciled to God by the death of his Son, it is certain that we are righteous before God, and that whatever we do, it pleases him. And although there are certain remnants of sin yet still in us, they are not laid to our charge, but pardoned for Christ's sake.

Apply

Are you clear in your own mind that simply by trusting in Christ alone you do not need to fear God's Judgment Day? If not, who could help you to think more about this?

Jesus has delivered us from servitude to the law and sin, but do you feel the pull of those things in your heart still?

Pray

Praise the Lord Jesus that he has set us free from the slavery of sin and fear of judgment.

Ask God to help you not to voluntarily return to the slavery of the law and of the devil.

Notes and prayers

✵ Day 16 ✵

Freedom to Love

GALATIANS 5:7–15

Some people carelessly turn the liberty of the Spirit into wanton sensuality, but they have lost Christ and Christian liberty and become slaves of the devil.

Read Galatians 5:7–15

What can you tell about the situation in the Galatian churches from this passage?

Why is spiritual freedom not just about 'doing whatever I like' (verses 13–15)?

Satan's abuse of grace

This evil is common and the most pernicious of all the evils that Satan stirs up in the doctrine of faith: namely, that in very many people he turns this liberty, by which Christ has made us free, into the liberty of the flesh. The apostle Jude also complains about this in his epistle: 'For certain individuals,' he says, 'whose condemnation was written about long ago have secretly slipped in among you. They are ungodly people, who pervert the grace of our God into a licence for immorality' (Jude 4).

For the flesh is utterly ignorant of the doctrine of grace – that is to say, it does not know that we are made righteous not by works but by faith only, and that the law has no authority over us. Therefore when it hears the doctrine of faith, it abuses it and turns it into sensuality, and by and by thus it reasons, 'If we are without law, let us then live as we want, let us do no good, let us give nothing to the needy, and let us not suffer any evil for there is no law to constrain us or bind us to do so'.

Liberty to love, not lust

So there is danger on either side; albeit the one is more tolerable then the other. If grace or faith are not preached, no one can be saved – for it is faith alone which justifies and saves. On the other side, if faith is preached (as of necessity it must be), the majority of people understand the doctrine of faith carnally, and turn the liberty of the Spirit into the liberty of the flesh.

All boast themselves to be professors of the gospel, and all boast of Christian liberty; and yet serving their own lusts, they give themselves to covetousness, pleasures, pride, envy and such other vices. No one does their duty faithfully; no one charitably serves the needs of their brother. The grief of this makes me sometimes so impatient!

Apply

What would you say to someone who said justification by faith alone undermines any need for Christians to live moral lives?

In your own heart, do you sometimes excuse your own sins on the basis that you are saved by faith alone and not by works?

Pray

Confess to God any times when you may have turned the grace of the gospel into an opportunity for sin, or have been tempted to.

Ask God to help you love your neighbour as yourself, not as a way of being saved but as a way of using your freedom to please him.

Notes and Prayers

�֍ Day 17 �֍

Spiritual Battle

GALATIANS 5:16–26

No Christian should be dismayed or discouraged when they feel in themselves the battle of the flesh against the Spirit.

Read Galatians 5:16–26

What do you think it means to 'live by the Spirit' (verse 16)?

What is the opposite of that?

Flesh and Spirit

Let no one despair if they feel the flesh often stirring up a new battle against the Spirit, or if they cannot quickly subdue the flesh and make it obedient to the Spirit. I also wish myself to have a more valiant and constant heart, which might be able boldly to scorn the threatenings of tyrants, the heresies and tumults which Satan and his soldiers (the enemies of the gospel) stir up. But also that I might soon shake off the vexations and anguish of spirit and might not fear the sharpness of death, but receive and embrace it as a most friendly guest. Others also wrestle with temptations and trials such as poverty, reproach, impatience, and such like.

When you feel this battle, resist in spirit and say, 'I am a sinner, and I feel sin in me, for I have not yet put off the flesh, in which sins dwells so long as it lives. But I will obey the Spirit and not the flesh – that is, I will by faith and hope lay hold on Christ, and by his word I will raise myself up, and will not fulfil the desire of the flesh.'

Holy desperation

I remember that Dr. Staupitius (*Luther's spiritual supervisor when he was a monk*) used to say, 'I have vowed to God a thousand times that I would become a better man. But I never performed that which I vowed. From now on, I will make no such vow, for I have now learned by experience that I am not able to perform it. Unless, therefore, God is favourable and merciful to me for Christ's sake, I shall not be able with all my vows and all my good deeds, to stand before him.'

This was not only a true, but also a godly and a holy desperation – and all those who want to be saved must confess this with heart and mouth. But let not those who feel the lust of the flesh despair of their salvation; because the more godly someone is, the more they will feel that battle.

Apply

When you next feel the battle between the flesh and the Spirit, will you give in or resist?

What would you say to someone who said they did not experience an internal battle such as Paul describes?

Pray

Pray for the Spirit's strength to enable you to keep waging war against the flesh.

Pray for the fruit of the Spirit (verses 22–23) to be more and more evident in your life as you fight.

Notes and Prayers

❊ Day 18 ❊

Greedy for Glory

Galatians 6:1–6

Paul rebukes the vanity of those who deceive themselves that they are 'something', when really they are not.

Read Galatians 6:1–6

Why do the people described here need to be careful in how they think of themselves?

What might indicate that Paul is talking here especially to those who minister to others?

The poison of vainglory

Although it may be understood of the works of this life or civil conversation, yet principally the apostle speaks here of the work of ministry, and denounces those vainglorious heads who, with their fantastical opinions, do trouble well-instructed consciences.

Those who are infected with this poison of vainglory have no regard whether their work – that is to say, their ministry – is pure, simple and faithful or not. But this alone they seek, that they may have the praise of the people. So the false apostles, when they saw that Paul preached the gospel purely to the Galatians, and that they could not bring any better doctrine, they began to find fault with those things which he had faithfully taught them. By this subtlety they won the favour of the Galatians, and made them hate Paul.

Bewitching the people

The proud and vainglorious join these three vices together. First, they are greedy for glory. Secondly, they are marvellously witty and wily in finding fault with other people's doings and sayings, in order to purchase the love, the approval and the praise of the people. And thirdly, when they have made a name for themselves, they become so stout and full of stomach that they dare venture upon all things. Therefore they are pernicious and pestilent fellows, whom I hate even with my very heart – 'for everyone looks out for their own interests, not those of Jesus Christ' (Philippians 2:21).

Against such people, Paul speaks here. Such vainglorious spirits teach the gospel so that they may win praise and estimation among people, that they may be counted excellent teachers. And when they have achieved this estimation, then they begin to rebuke the sayings and doings of others, and highly commend their own. By this subtlety they bewitch the minds of the people, who, because they have itching ears, are not only delighted with new opinions but also rejoice to see those teachers which they had before being abased and defaced by these new upstarts and glorious heads – and all because they loathe the word.

Apply

Do you think too highly of yourself and your spirituality, abilities or ministry?

Are you 'marvellously witty and wily in finding fault with other people's doings and sayings'?

Pray

Confess to God if you have been too quick to criticise others to build your own reputation or if you are 'greedy for glory'.

Ask God to help you root out pride and vainglory from your own life.

Notes and prayers

❋ DAY 19 ❋

Gospel Liberality

GALATIANS 6:6–10

Those who sow to please the Spirit will be blessed both in this life and the life to come, but those who wearily sow to the flesh will be accursed both now and in the future.

Read Galatians 6:6–10

What's in it for us if we do good works?

Why should we persist in them and not grow weary?

Funding ministry

Here Paul preaches to the hearers of the word, commanding them to bestow all good things upon those who have taught and instructed them in the word. I have sometimes marvelled why the apostle commanded the churches so diligently to nourish their teachers. For within the Roman Catholic church I saw that everyone gave abundantly to the building and maintaining of lavish temples, and to the increase of the revenues of those who were appointed to their service.

Therefore I thought that Paul had commanded this in vain, seeing that all manner of good things were not only abundantly given to the clergy, but they also overflowed in wealth and riches. But now I know the cause why they had such abundance before, and why the pastors and ministers of the word are now in want.

For Satan can abide nothing less than the light of the gospel. Therefore when he sees that it begins to shine, he rages and goes about with all his might to quench it. And this he attempts two ways: first by lying spirits and force of tyrants; and then by poverty and famine. But because he could not oppress the gospel in this country (praised be God) by heretics and tyrants, he attempted to withdraw the livings of the ministers, so that they should forsake the ministry – and the miserable people being destitute of the word of God should become in time like savage, wild beasts.

Generosity to all

The apostle then passes from the particular to the general, and exhorts people generally to all good works. As if he should say, 'Let us be liberal and bountiful, not only towards the ministers of the word, but also towards all others – and that without weariness'. For it is an easy matter for someone to do good once or twice; but to continue and not be discouraged through the ingratitude of others, that is very hard. But in due time we shall reap. Wait and look for the harvest that is to come, and then no ingratitude will be able to pluck you away from well doing.

Apply

Are you generous in supporting the gospel ministry from which you benefit?

Have you grown weary in being generous to others, and do you need to remember the heavenly reward for good and faithful servants?

Pray

Pray for there to be sufficient finance to train and support more gospel ministers in your area.

Ask God to give you opportunities and strength to 'do good to all people, especially to those who belong to the family of believers'.

Notes and prayers

❋ Day 20 ❋

Crucified to the World

GALATIANS 6:11–18

Our glory is a different kind of glory from that which the world values. We rejoice in suffering, persecution and death; but they boast in power, riches and honour.

Read Galatians 6:11–18

What does Paul say his opponents in Galatia were most interested in (verses 12–13)?

What was Paul most interested in (verses 14–15)?

Damning the world

This is Paul's manner of speaking: 'The world has been crucified to me' – that is, *I judge the world to be damned*. 'And I [am crucified] to the world' – that is, *The world judges me to be damned*.

Thus we crucify and condemn one another. I abhor all the doctrine, righteousness, and works of the world as the poison of the devil. The world detests my doctrine and deeds, and judges me to be a seditious, a pernicious, a pestilential fellow, and a heretic.

So, at this day, the world is crucified to us, and we to the world. We curse and condemn all human traditions concerning masses, holy orders, vows, works, and all the abominations of heretics, as the dirt of the devil. They in return persecute and kill us as destroyers of religion and troublers of the public peace.

The monks dreamed that the world was crucified to them when they entered into their monasteries. But by this means Christ is crucified and not the world. Indeed, the world is delivered from being crucified, and is the more quickened, by that opinion of holiness and trust which religious people had in their own righteousness. Most foolishly and wickedly therefore was this sentence of the apostle twisted to be about entering into monasteries.

Judging rightly

Paul speaks here of a high matter, of great importance. That is to say, what every faithful person judges to be the wisdom, righteousness and power of God, the world condemns as the greatest folly, wickedness and weakness. And on the other side, that which the world judges to be the highest religion and service of God, the faithful know to be nothing else but lamentable and horrible blasphemy against God.

Now, in the Scriptures, 'the world' not only signifies ungodly and wicked people, but the very best, the wisest and holiest that are of the world. But the godly condemn the world, and the world condemns the godly. Yet the godly have the right judgment on their side.

Apply

Do you value what the world around you values, and care about what it cares about?

Do you care about 'impressing people by means of the flesh' more than you should?

Pray

Ask the Spirit to show you how you are adopting the values of the world instead of judging everything in the light of the cross.

Thank God for everything we have learned from Galatians, and from Martin Luther!

Notes and Prayers

Looking for your next Bible study?

REFLECTING ON...
Genesis

with *John Calvin*

'Reading the Bible is one of the highest joys in the Christian life. We know that, just as John Calvin did before us. This small study on Genesis is like reading the Bible with John Calvin alongside us in the room. The great French reformer trains us to be careful apprentices to Scripture, and as we do so, we enjoy seeing Christ and all his benefits wonderfully held out to us in the gospel.'

Mark Earngey,
Head of Church History, Moore Theological College, Sydney

Scripture with the Saints
Reading the Bible with faithful believers
across the ages

A MONTH with THE MESSIAH

Reflections on Handel's Masterpiece

Handel's Messiah has captivated audiences for centuries, but the depth of its theological and spiritual messages invites deeper exploration. In A Month with the Messiah, a cast of thirty scholars, pastors, musicians, and theologians come together to provide a profound and accessible devotional commentary on this musical masterpiece. Curated to appeal both to long-time admirers and newcomers, this book dives into the libretto's scriptural themes with clarity and reverence.

This beautifully produced hardback companion to the Messiah invites readers on a journey of spiritual reflection, exploring the hope, redemption, and joy that Handel's music captures so vividly. Each contributor brings a unique perspective, drawing from their rich backgrounds to shed light on how these passages resonate in today's world.

Whether you're enjoying Messiah for the first time or looking to deepen your appreciation of it, this collection is a companion to enrich your listening, worship, and reflection on Handel's enduring work.

Perfect as a book for Advent, as a Christmas gift for someone else, or for your own enjoyment!

£14.99 Hardback, £9.99 digital

Order direct from Church Society:

www.churchsociety.org | admin@churchsociety.org
+44 1923 255410

Church Society

Church Society

offering strategic leadership

For more than 180 years, Church Society has been contending to reform and renew the Church of England in biblical faith, on the basis of its Reformed foundations as expressed in the doctrine of the Articles, the worship of the Prayer Book, and the ministry of the Ordinal.

To find out more and to join Church Society, please visit our website, churchsociety.org

resourcing today's church

Church Society publishes several new books each year, bringing the best of our Anglican Evangelical heritage to new generations, and responding to new pressures and opportunities in today's Church and nation. We also produce a weekly podcast, a quarterly magazine and a theological journal, as well as our regular blog.

serving tomorrow's church

As part of our commitment to raising up a new generation of leaders, we host the annual Junior Anglican Evangelical Conference for those in the early stages of ministry. Church Society also has patronage of around 130 parishes, helping to protect evangelical ministry in the Church of England for the future.